D0504053

Bass
Rock Songbook

INTRODUCTION

Welcome to FastTrack™!

Hope you are ready to play some hits. Have you and your friends formed a band? Or do you feel like soloing with the CD? Either way, make sure you're relaxed and comfortable... it's time to play!

As always, don't try to bite off more than you can chew. If your fingers hurt, take some time off. If you get frustrated, put down your bass, relax and just listen to the CD. If you forget a note position or rhythmic value, go back and learn it. If you're doing fine, think about charging admission.

CONTENTS

ABOUT THE CD

Each song in the book is included on the CD, so you can hear how it sounds and play along when you're ready.

Each example on the CD is preceded by one measure of "clicks" to indicate the tempo and meter. Pan right to hear the bass part emphasized. Pan left to hear the accompaniment emphasized.

ISBN 978-1-4234-9573-4

HAL•LEONARD®
CORPORATION

7777 W. BLUEMOUND RD. P.O. BOX 13819 MILWAUKEE, WI 53213

Visit Hal Leonard Online at
www.halleonard.com

LEARN SOMETHING NEW EACH DAY

We know you're eager to play, but first we need to explain a few new things. We'll make it brief—only one page...

Melody and Lyrics

The additional musical staff on top shows you the song's melody and lyrics. This way, you can follow along more easily as you play your accompaniment part, whether you're playing, resting or showing off with a solo... well, sometimes bass players do get a solo.

And if you happen to be playing with a singer, this staff is their part.

Endings

1st and 2nd Endings

These are indicated by brackets and numbers:

Simply play the song through to the first ending, then repeat back to the first repeat sign, or beginning of the song (whichever is the case). Play through the song again, but skip the first ending and play the second ending.

D.S. al Coda

When you see these words, go back and repeat from this symbol: 𝄋

Play until you see the words "To Coda" then skip to the Coda, indicated by this symbol: 𝄌

Now just finish the song.

That's about it! Enjoy the music...

◆ Are You Gonna Be My Girl

Words and Music by Cameron Muncey and Nicholas Cester

Intro
Fast Rock ♩ = 206

N.C.

1.

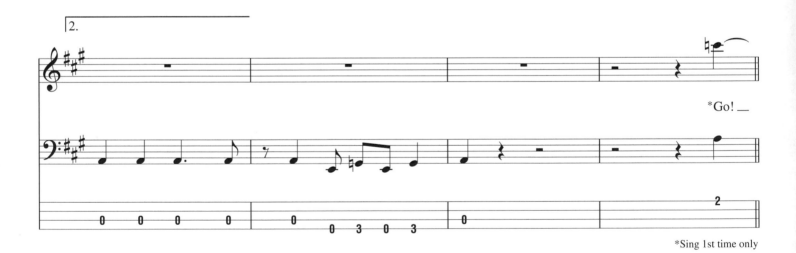

2.

*Go! __

*Sing 1st time only

A

1. So,
2. Well, it's a

Verse

one, two, three, take my hand and come with me be-cause you look so fine and I

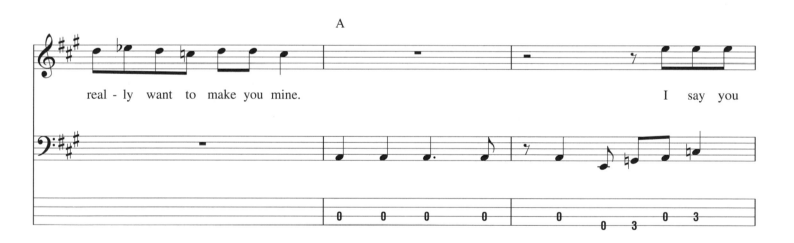

real-ly want to make you mine. I say you

look so fine and I real-ly want to make you mine.

Well, four, five, six, come on ____ and get your kicks. Now you

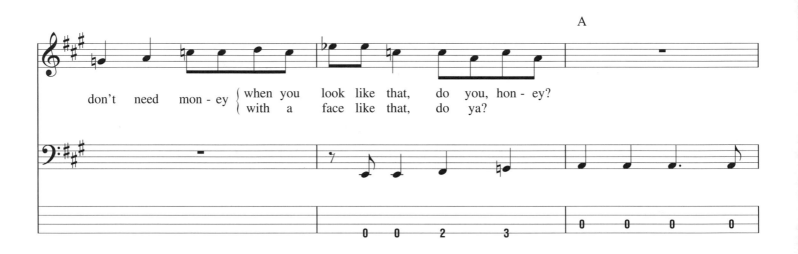

don't need mon-ey { when you look like that, do you, hon-ey?
                    with a face like that, do ya?

Pre-Chorus

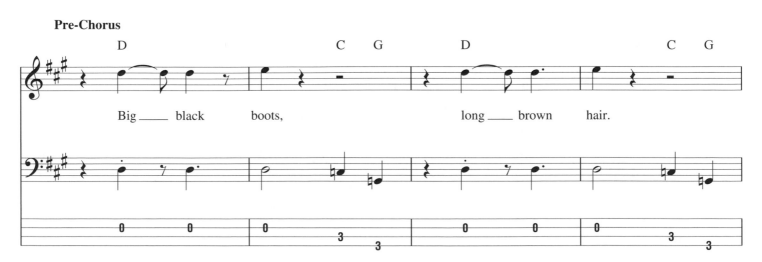

Big ____ black boots, long ____ brown hair.

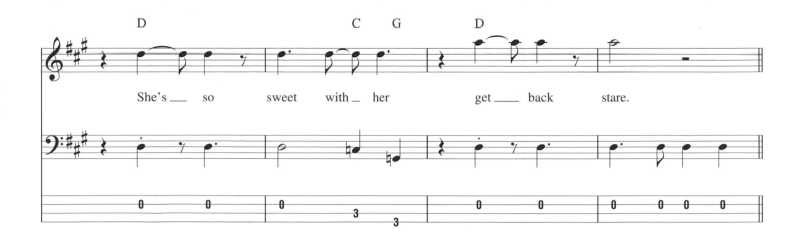

She's __ so sweet with __ her get __ back stare.

𝄋 Chorus

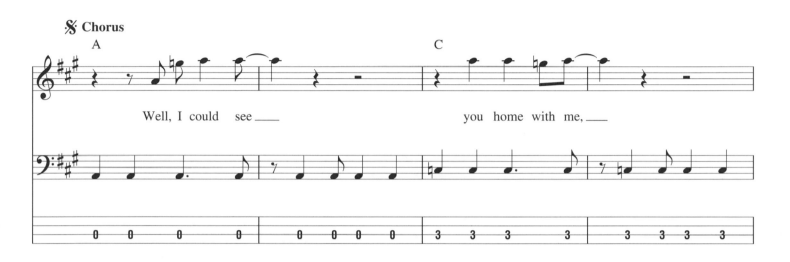

Well, I could see ___ you home with me, ___

but you were with __ an - oth - er man, _____ yeah. __

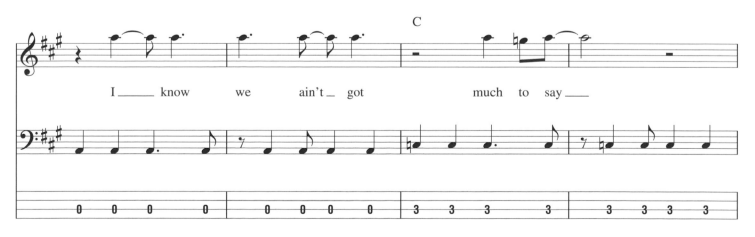

I _____ know we ain't __ got much to say ___

be - fore I let___ you get a - way,_____ yeah.___

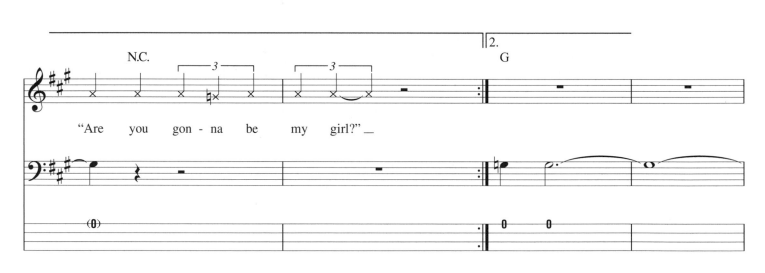

I said,

"Are you gon - na be my girl?" __

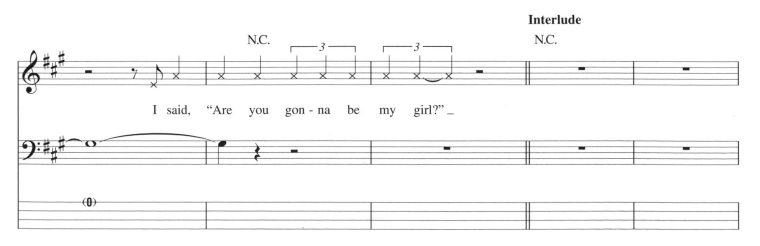

Interlude

I said, "Are you gon - na be my girl?" _

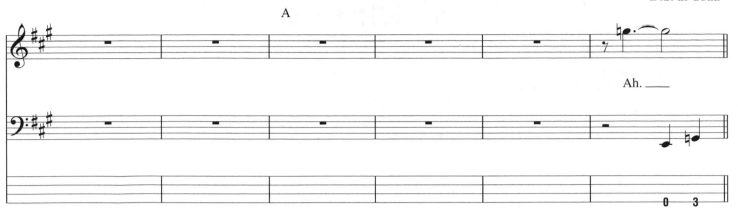

A

Ah. ____

Coda

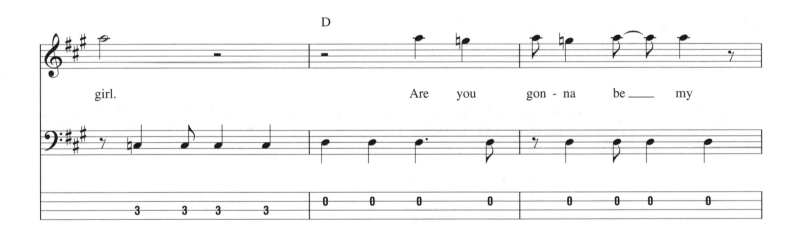

C

Uh, be my girl. ____ Be ____ my

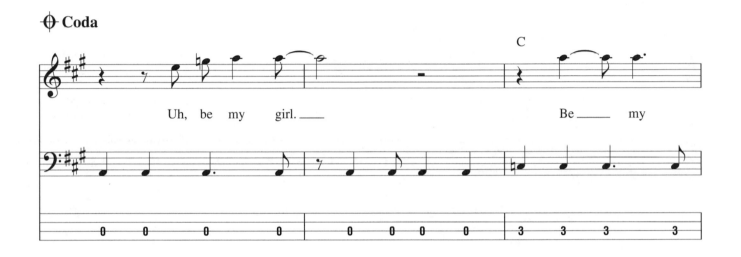

D

girl. Are you gon - na be ____ my

A G D

girl? _____ Yeah! _____

◆② Clocks

Words and Music by Guy Berryman, Jon Buckland, Will Champion and Chris Martin

1. Lights go out and I can't be saved. _ Tides that I tried to
2. Con - fu - sion _ nev - er stops. _ Clos - ing _ walls and

swim a - gainst _ brought me down up - on my knees. _
tick - ing clocks _ gon - na come back and take you home. _ I

Oh, I beg, I beg and plead. _ Sing - in': come out of
could not stop that you now know. _ Sing - in': come out up -

things un - said. ___ / on my seas, ___ Shoot an ap - ple off my head. ___ / curse missed op - por - tu - ni - ties. ___ And a / Am I

trou - ble that can't be named. ___ / a part ___ of the cure ___ A tig - er's wait - ing to be tamed. ___ / or am I part of the dis - ease? ___ Sing-in':

Chorus

You ___ are. ___

To Coda ⊕

You ___ are. ___

11

Interlude

2nd time, D.S. al Coda

⊕ Coda

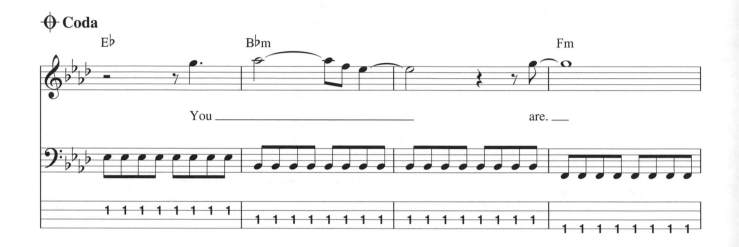

You _____ are. __

You _____ are. __

Bridge

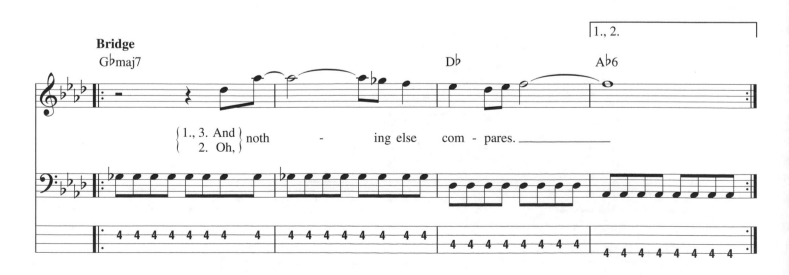

{ 1., 3. And }
{ 2. Oh, } noth - ing else com - pares. _____

◆ Dani California

Words and Music by Anthony Kiedis, Flea, John Frusciante and Chad Smith

Intro
Moderately ♩ = 96

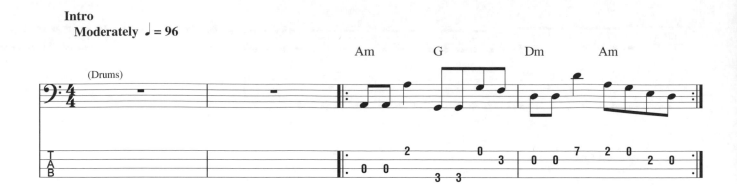

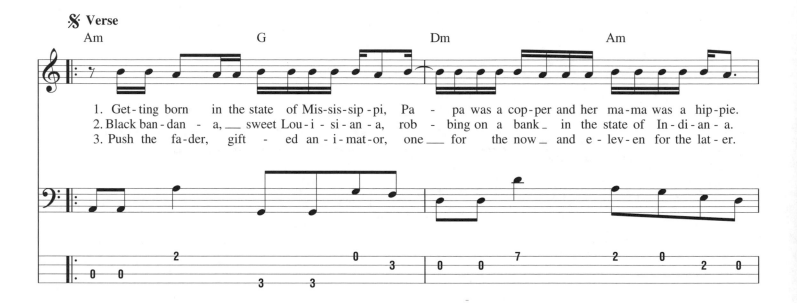

1. Get-ting born   in the state of Mis-sis-sip-pi, Pa — pa was a cop-per and her ma-ma was a hip-pie.
2. Black ban-dan — a, — sweet Lou-i-si-an-a, rob - bing on a bank — in the state of In-di-an - a.
3. Push the fa-der, gift - ed an-i-mat-or, one — for the now — and e-lev-en for the lat - er.

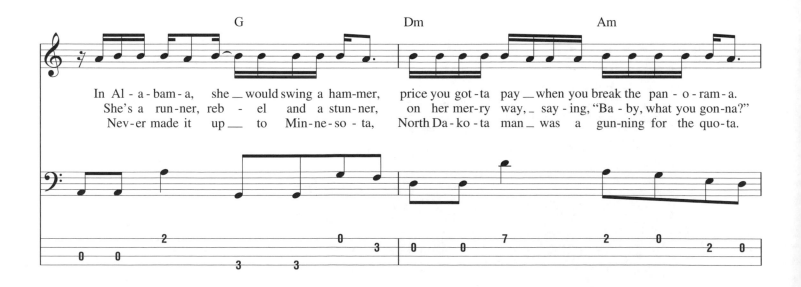

In Al-a-bam-a, she — would swing a ham-mer, price you got-ta pay — when you break the pan-o-ram-a.
She's a run-ner, reb - el and a stun-ner, on her mer-ry way, — say-ing, "Ba - by, what you gon-na?"
Nev-er made it up — to Min-ne-so-ta, North Da-ko-ta man — was a gun-ning for the quo-ta.

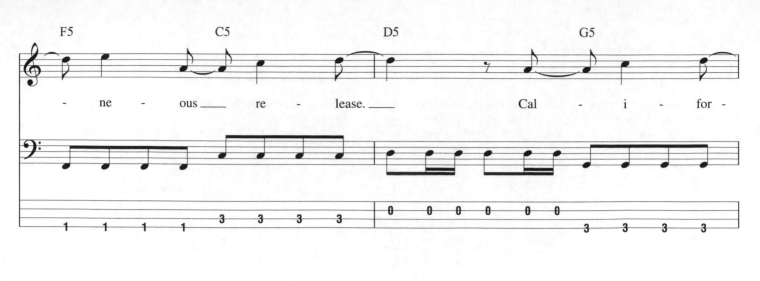

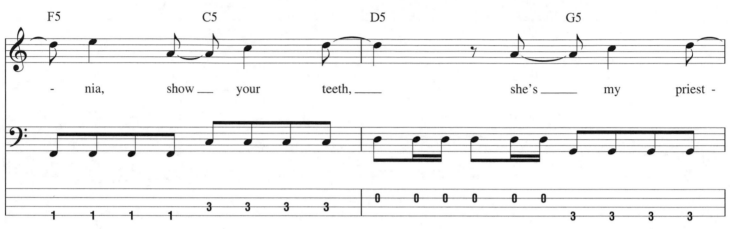

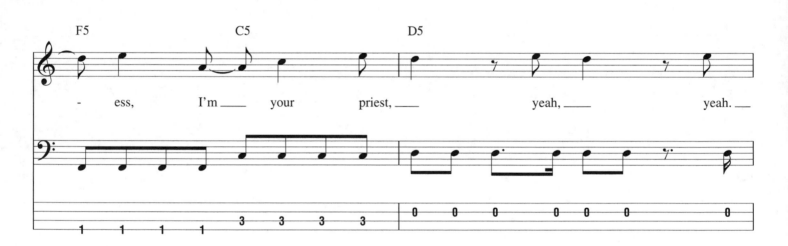

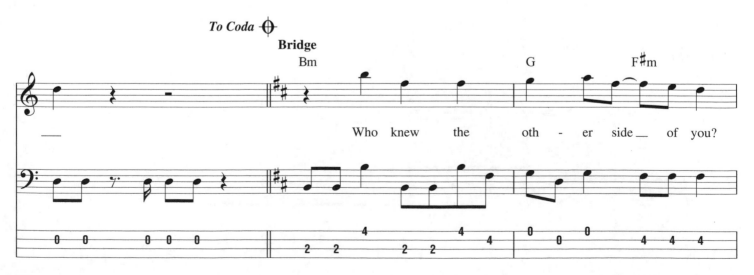

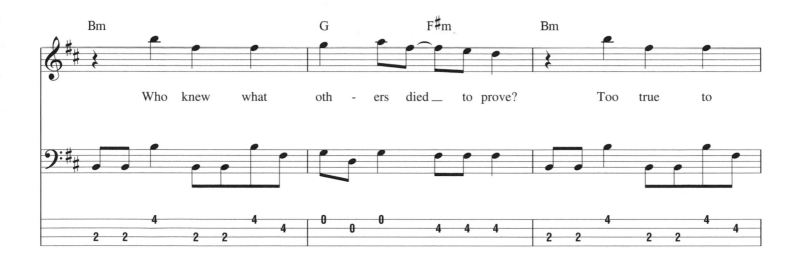

Who knew what oth - ers died — to prove? Too true to

D.S. al Coda
(take 2nd ending)

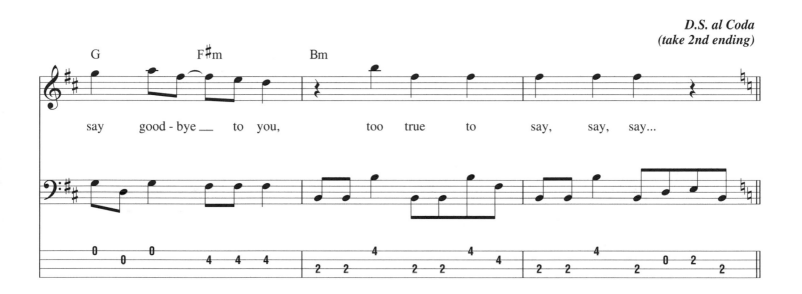

say good - bye — to you, too true to say, say, say...

⊕ Coda

Outro

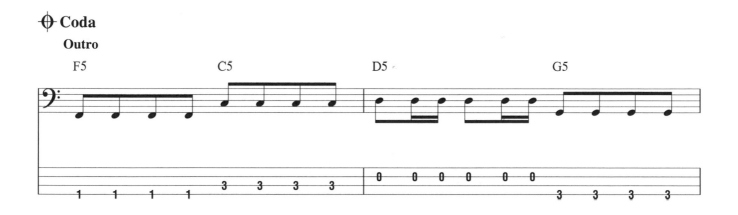

◆4 Gives You Hell

Words and Music by Tyson Ritter and Nick Wheeler

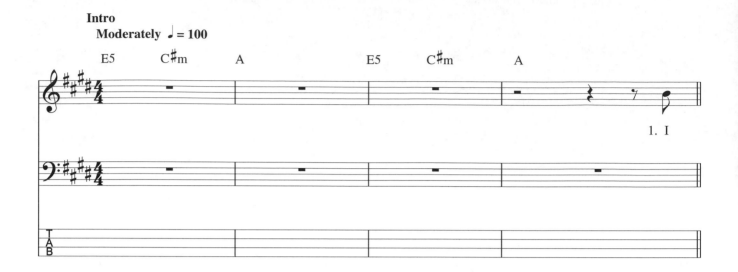

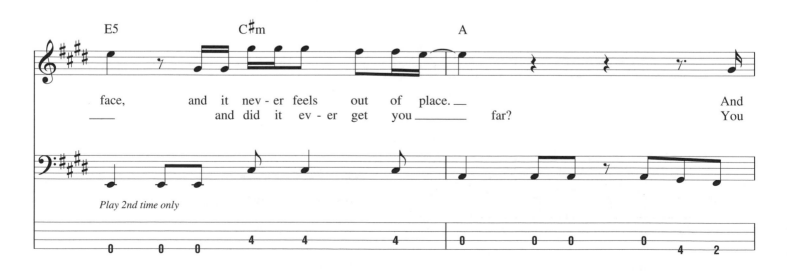

Pre-Chorus

truth be told, __ I miss __ you. And truth be told, I'm ly-

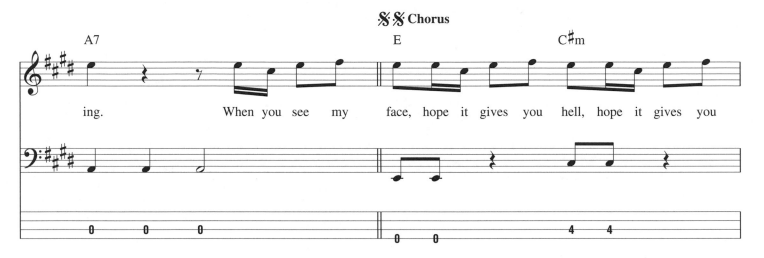

Chorus

ing. When you see my face, hope it gives you hell, hope it gives you

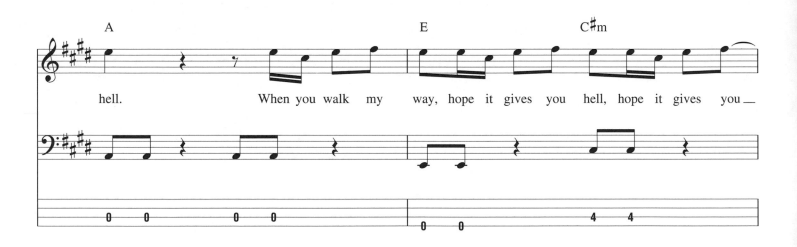

hell. When you walk my way, hope it gives you hell, hope it gives you __

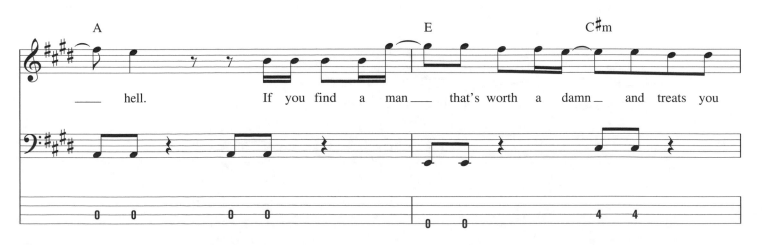

__ hell. If you find a man __ that's worth a damn __ and treats you

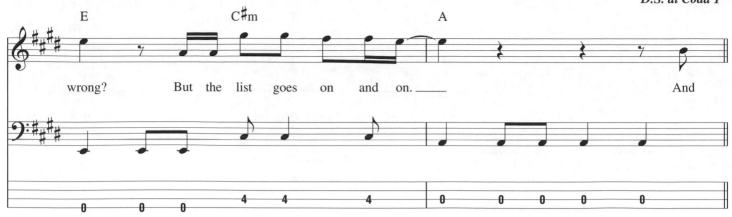

wrong?   But the list goes on and on.____   And

Coda 1

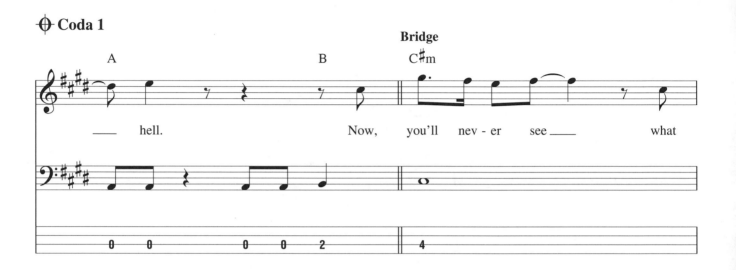

____ hell.   Now,   you'll nev - er   see ____   what

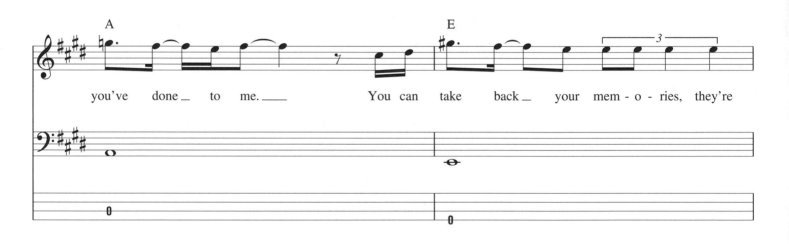

you've done __ to me. ____   You can take back __ your mem - o - ries, they're

no good __ to me. ____   And here's to all ____ your lies, ____   you can

look me in the eyes with the sad, sad look that you

D.S.S. al Coda 2

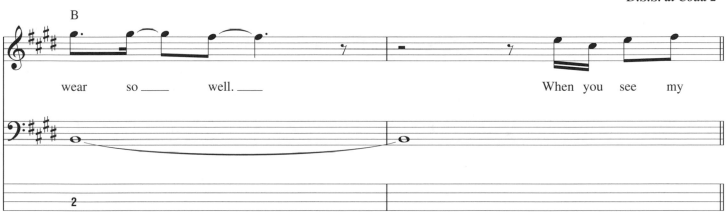

wear so well. When you see my

◈ **Coda 2**

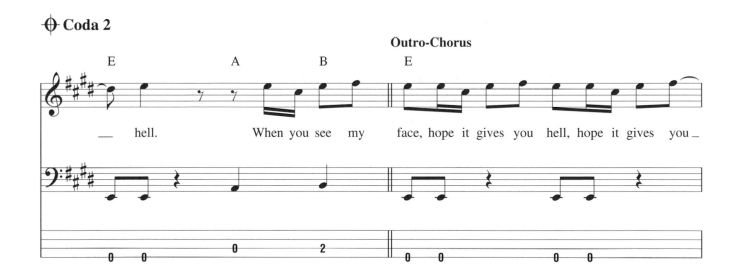

Outro-Chorus

hell. When you see my face, hope it gives you hell, hope it gives you

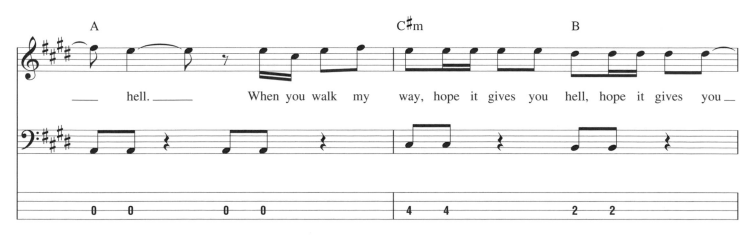

hell. When you walk my way, hope it gives you hell, hope it gives you

E

— hell.　　When you hear this　song　and you sing　a - long, —　but you nev - er　tell, —

A　　　　　　　　　　　　　　C#m　　　　　　　　B

— 　　then you're the　fool.　I'm just　as　well, hope it gives　you

song, I hope that it will give you

1.

E

hell.　　When you hear　this　hell.

2.

E

You can sing a -

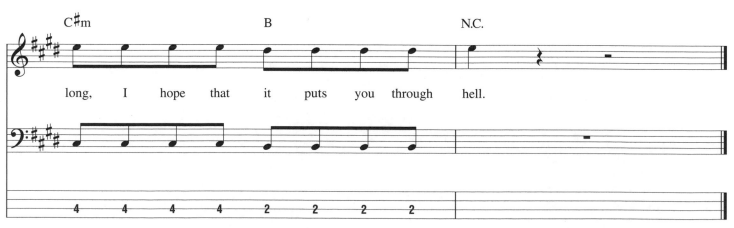

C#m　　　　　　　　B　　　　　　　　N.C.

long, I hope that it puts you through hell.

Grenade

**Words and Music by Bruno Mars, Ari Levine, Philip Lawrence,
Christopher Steven Brown, Claude Kelly and Andrew Wyatt**

Intro

Moderately fast ♩ = 111

1. Eas-y come, eas-y go; that's just how you live. Oh, take, take, take it all, but you nev-er give.

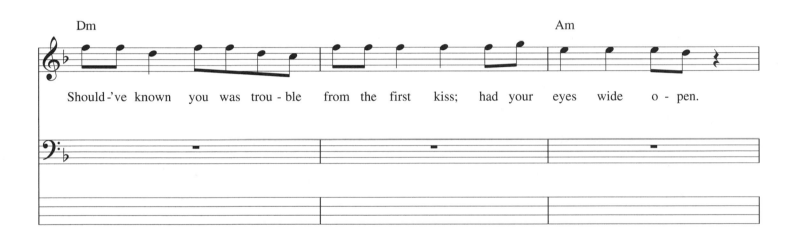

Should-'ve known you was trou-ble from the first kiss; had your eyes wide o-pen.

℅ Pre-Chorus

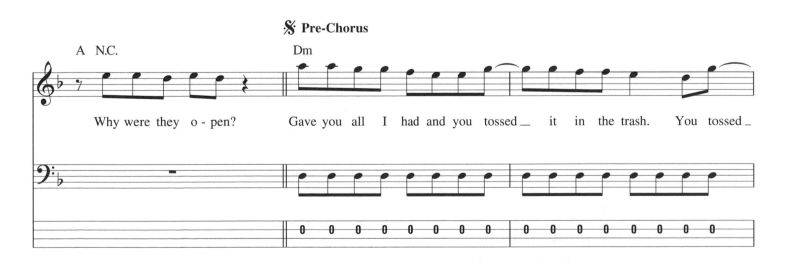

Why were they o-pen? Gave you all I had and you tossed it in the trash. You tossed

_____ it in the trash; you did. _____ To give _____ me all your love is all _____

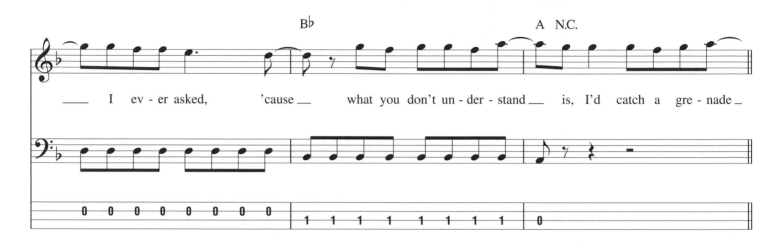

_____ I ev - er asked, 'cause _____ what you don't un - der - stand _____ is, I'd catch a gre - nade _____

𝄋 𝄋 Chorus

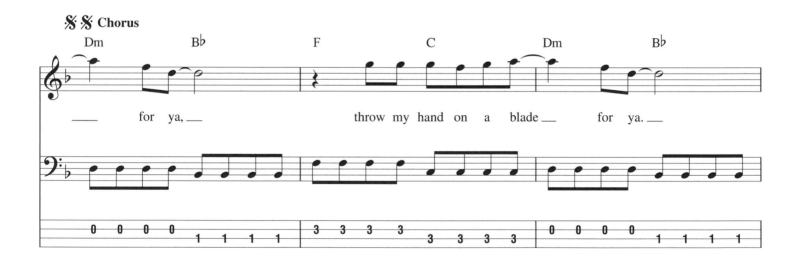

_____ for ya, _____ throw my hand on a blade _____ for ya. _____

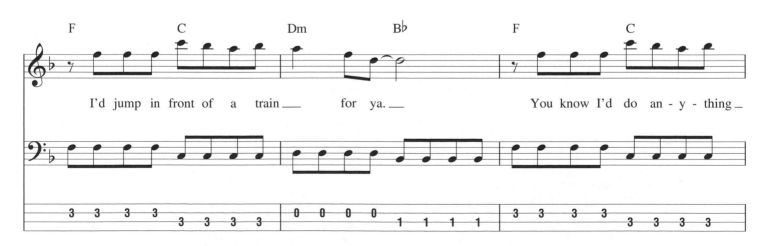

I'd jump in front of a train _____ for ya. _____ You know I'd do an - y - thing _____

dev-il I said, "Hey," when you get back to where you're from. Mad wom-an, bad wom-an;

D.S. al Coda 1

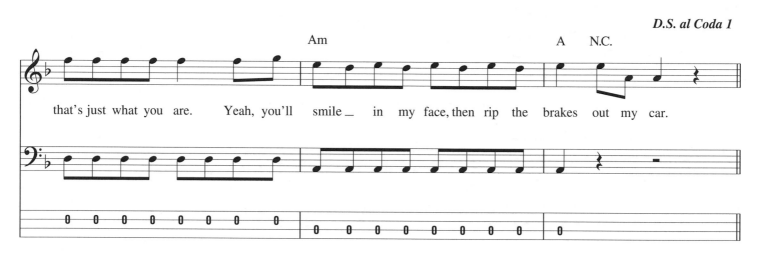

that's just what you are. Yeah, you'll smile ___ in my face, then rip the brakes out my car.

Coda 1

Bridge

If my bod-y was on fi-re,

ooh, you'd watch me burn down in flames. You said you

21 Guns

**Words and Music by David Bowie, John Phillips,
Billie Joe Armstrong, Mike Pritchard and Frank Wright**

Verse

2. When you're at the ___ end of the road ___ and you lost ___ all

sense of con - trol. ___ And your thoughts ___ have ___ tak - en their toll ___ when your

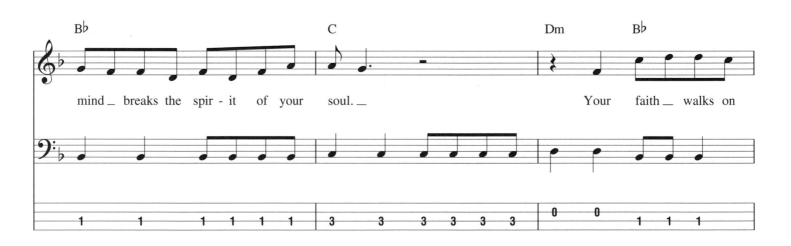

mind ___ breaks the spir - it of your soul. ___ Your faith ___ walks on

bro - ken glass ___ and the hang - o - ver does - n't pass. ___

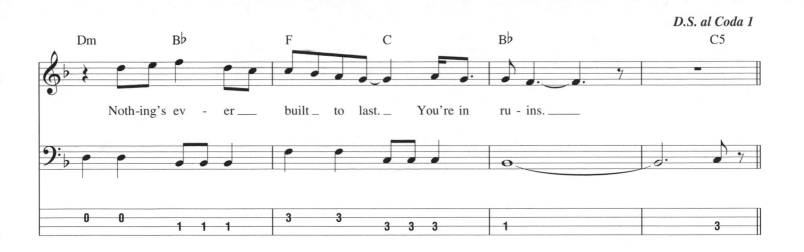

✛ Coda 1

Bridge

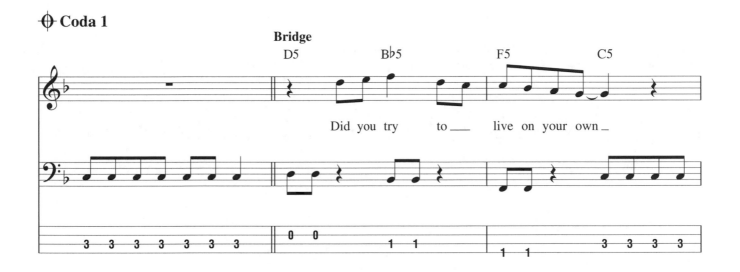

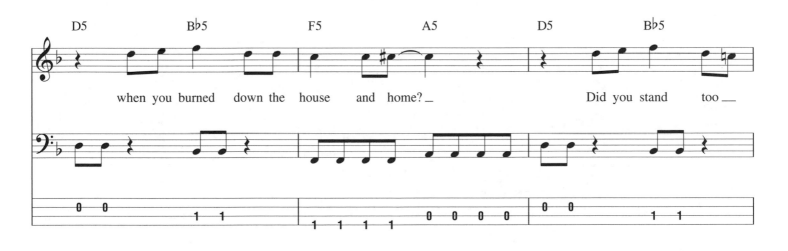

Guitar Solo

*Sing 1st time only.

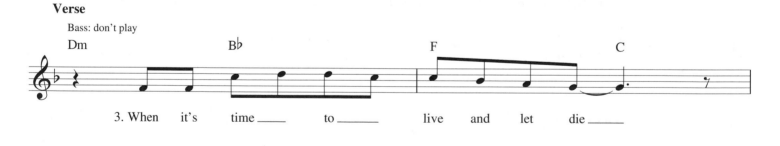

Interlude

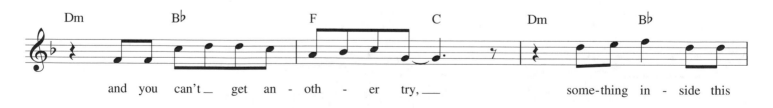

Verse

Bass: don't play

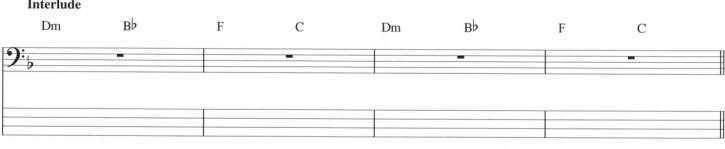

3. When it's time ___ to ___ live and let die ___

and you can't ___ get an - oth - er try, ___ some-thing in - side this

D.S. al Coda 2

heart ___ has died. ___ You're in ru - ins.

◆ Use Somebody

**Words and Music by Caleb Followill, Nathan Followill,
Jared Followill and Matthew Followill**

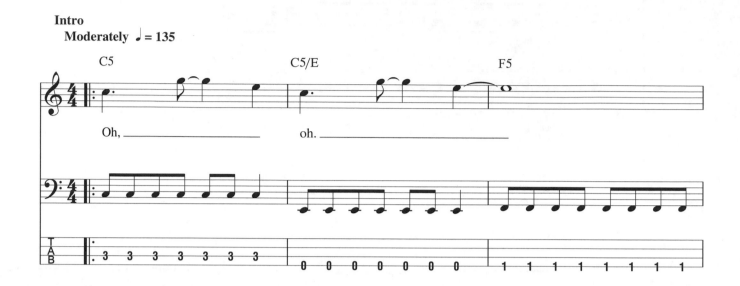

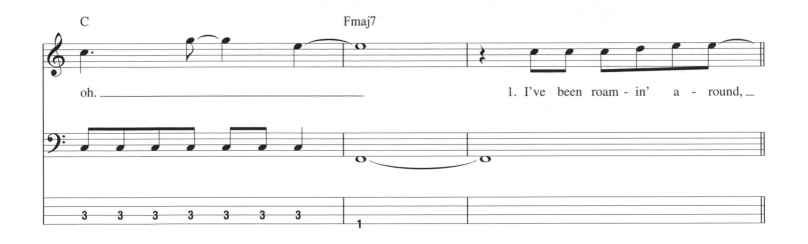

oh. _____ 1. I've been roam - in' a - round, _

Verse

Bass: don't play

___ I was look - in' down _____ at all ___ I see. ____

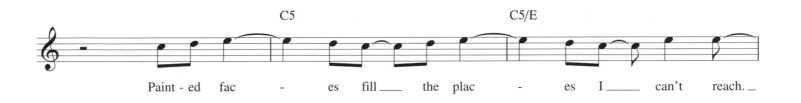

Paint - ed fac - es fill ___ the plac - es I ____ can't reach. _

___ You know __ that I could use some - bod - y. ____

___ You know __ that I could

use some - bod - y, _____

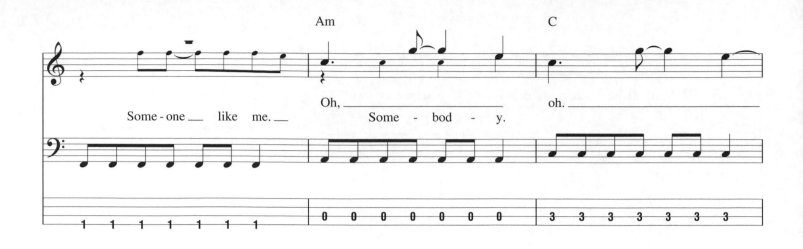

Some-one ___ like me. ___ Oh, _____ Some-bod-y. oh. _____

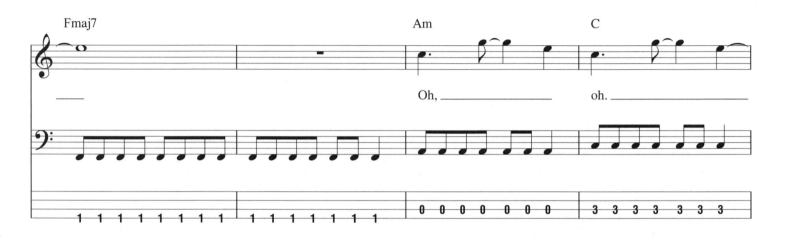

___ Oh, _____ oh. _____

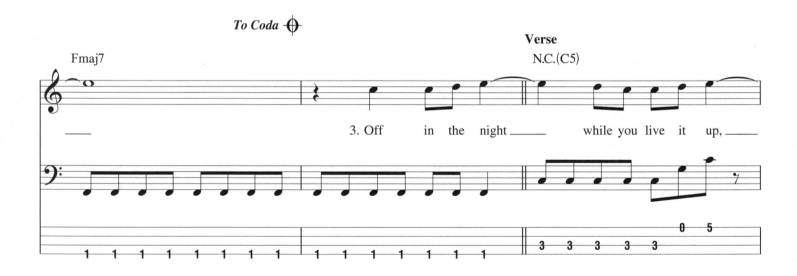

Verse

___ 3. Off in the night _____ while you live it up, _____

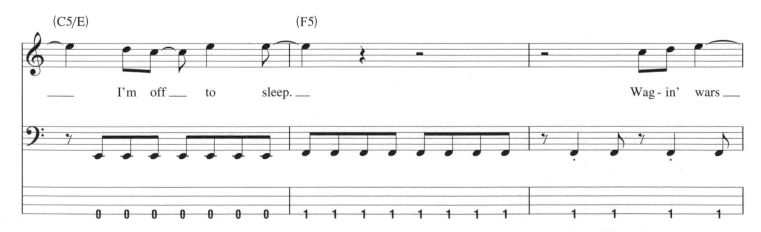

___ I'm off ___ to sleep. ___ Wag-in' wars ___

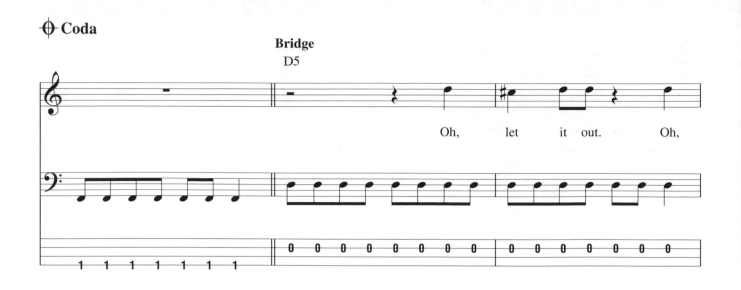

⊕ Coda

Bridge

Oh, let it out. Oh,

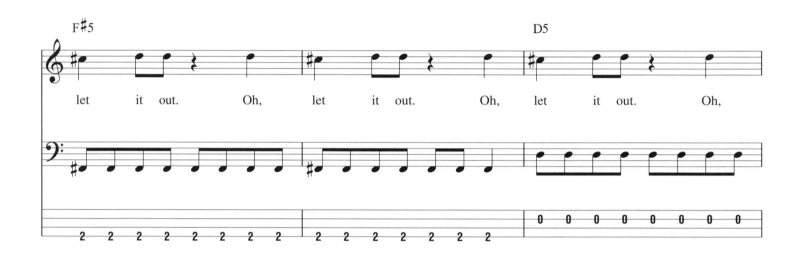

let it out. Oh, let it out. Oh, let it out. Oh,

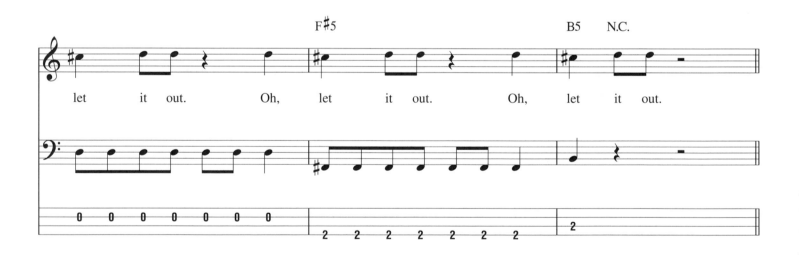

let it out. Oh, let it out. Oh, let it out.

Guitar Solo

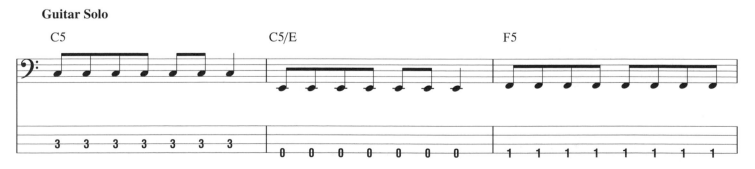

43

Home

Words and Music by Chris Daughtry

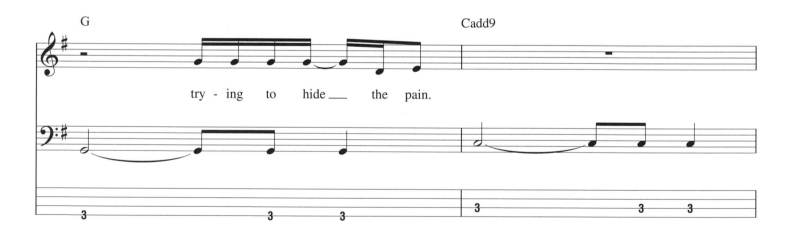

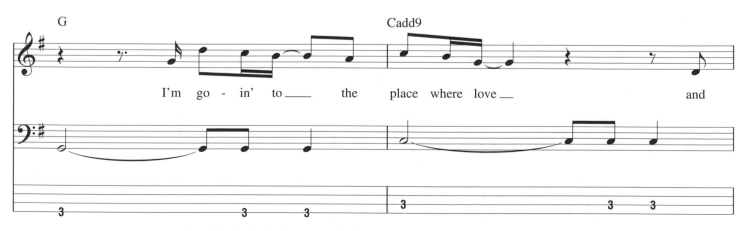

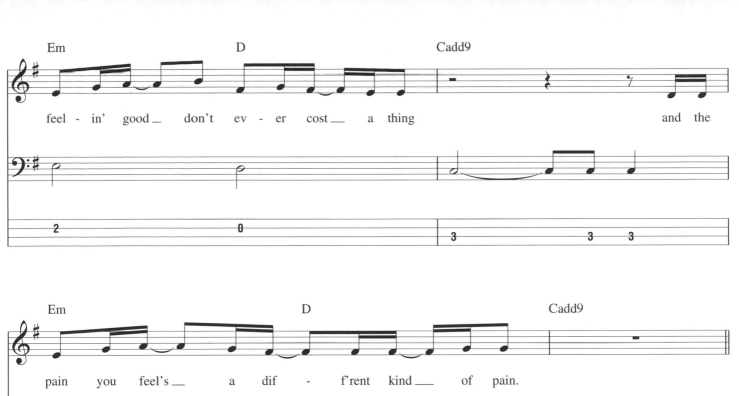

feel - in' good __ don't ev - er cost __ a thing

and the

pain you feel's __ a dif - f'rent kind __ of pain.

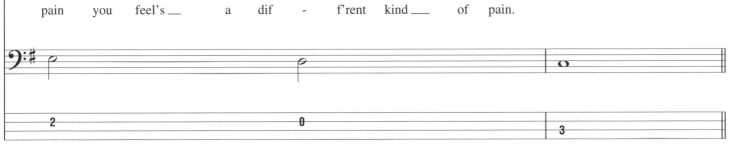

𝄋 **Chorus**

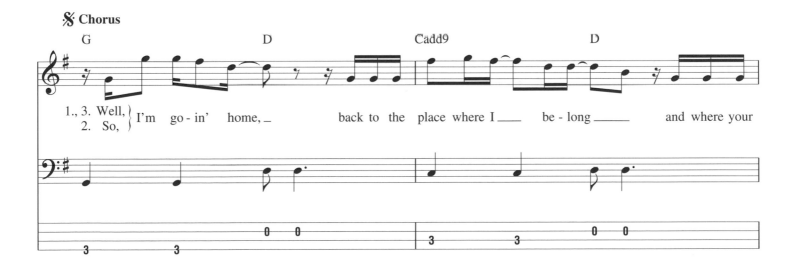

1., 3. Well,
2. So,
I'm go - in' home, __ back to the place where I __ be - long _____ and where your

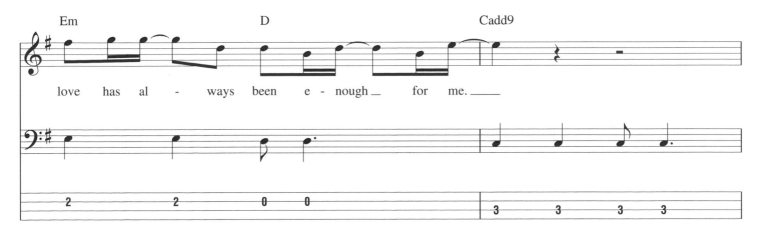

love has al - ways been e - nough __ for me. _____

45

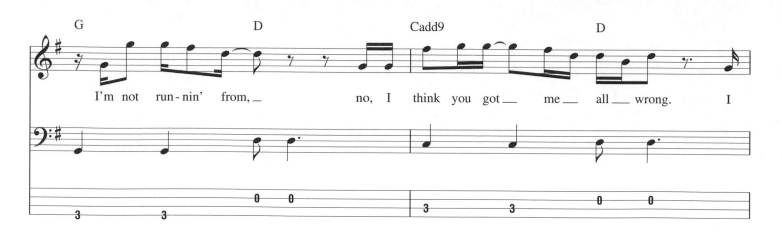

I'm not run-nin' from, ___ no, I think you got ___ me ___ all ___ wrong. I

don't re-gret ___ this life I chose ___ for me. ___ But these

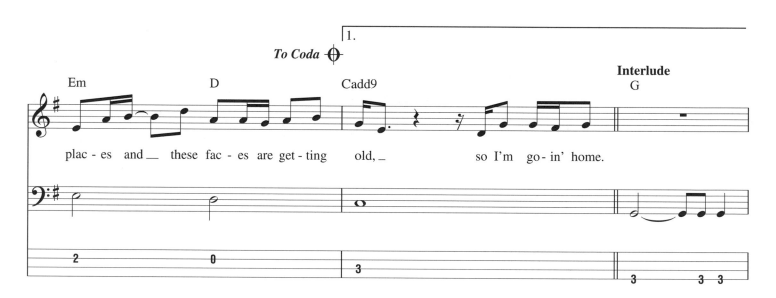

plac-es and ___ these fac-es are get-ting old, ___ so I'm go-in' home.

Well, I'm go-in' home.   old. ___

Bridge

Be care - ful what _ you wish for ____ 'cause you just might get it all. __

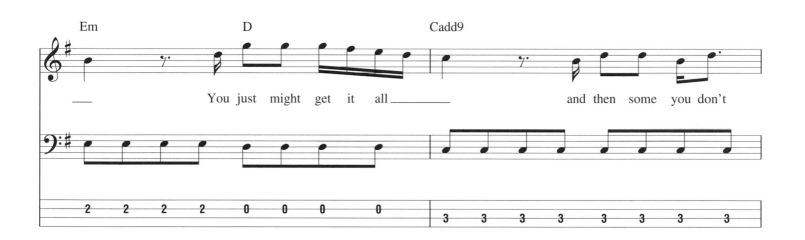

__ You just might get it all _____ and then some you don't

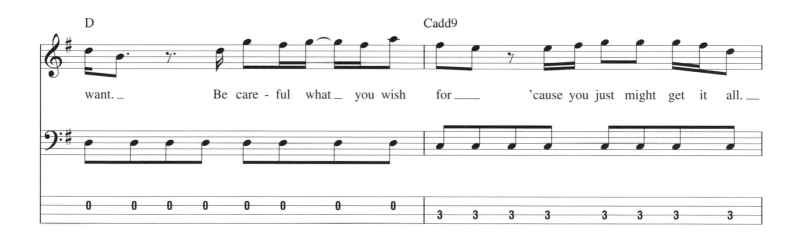

want. _ Be care - ful what _ you wish for ____ 'cause you just might get it all. __

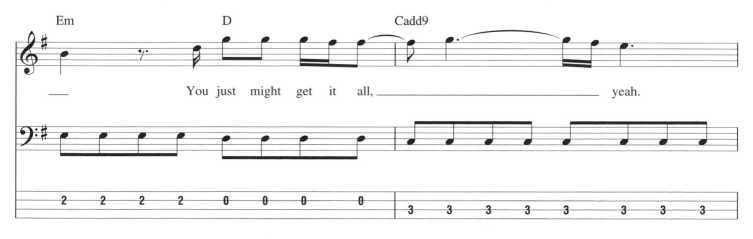

__ You just might get it all, _____ yeah.

D.S. al Coda
Em D Cadd9
Em D Cadd9
Coda
Cadd9
Em
D
old. I said, these plac - es and these fac - es are get - ting
Cadd9
Em D Cadd9
old, so I'm go - in' home.
Em D Cadd9
G
I'm go - in' home.

Additional Lyrics

2. The miles are getting longer, it seems,
   The closer I get to you.
   I've not always been the best man or friend for you,
   But your love remains true.
   And I don't know why
   You always seem to give me another try.

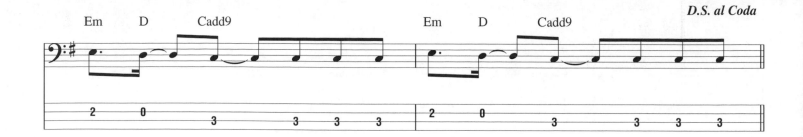

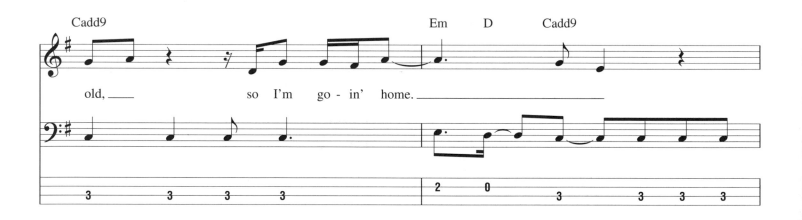

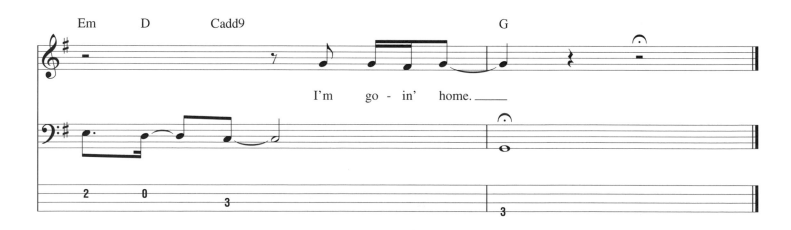